# Wrigglebottom

June Crebbin

Illustrated by Susan Hellard

CAMBRIDGE
UNIVERSITY PRESS

One morning, Max jumped out of bed.

He jumped down the stairs.

He hopped into the kitchen.

"Good morning, Max," said Mum.
"Come and have some breakfast."

Max sat down. But he couldn't sit still.
He wriggled and jiggled.

"Do sit still," said Mum. "You're making me dizzy. You're such a wrigglebottom."

At school, Max raced round the playground.

When the bell rang, he raced into school.

"Slow down, Max," said his
teacher, Miss Parker.

Max sat down. But he couldn't sit still.

He jumped up to fetch a pencil. Then he
fetched a rubber. Then he fetched a book.

"Do sit still," said Miss Parker.
"You're making me dizzy. You're such
a wrigglebottom."

At home-time, Max raced along the street.
He raced into his house.

He jumped up and down on the sofa.
Dad came home.
"I've got a surprise for you," he said.
"But you'll have to sit still."

Max sat down. He sat quite still.

"Good," said Dad.
He went out of the room and came
back with . . .

. . . a puppy!

"There," he said. He put the puppy on
Max's lap.

Max stroked the puppy gently. She was very sleepy. She lay on his lap.

"Thank you," said Max.

Suddenly, the puppy woke up. She licked
Max's face. She jumped up and down. She
wriggled and jiggled.

Max laughed.

"Do sit still," he said. "You're making me dizzy. You're such a wrigglebottom!"